What Do You Know About
The Age of Exploration?

PowerKiDS
press™
New York

Lynn George

Published in 2008 by The Rosen Publishing Group, Inc.
29 East 21st Street, New York, NY 10010

First Edition

Editor: Joanne Randolph
Book Design: Kate Laczynski

Photo Credits: Cover, pp. 1, 5, 9, 11–14, 16–18, 19 (bottom)–21 © Getty Images; pp. 6, 19 (top) © North Wind Picture Archives; pp. 7–8, 10, 15 Shutterstock.com.

Library of Congress Cataloging-in-Publication Data

George, Lynn.
  What do you know about the age of exploration? / Lynn George.
      p. cm. — (20 questions : history)
  Includes index.
  ISBN 978-1-4042-4190-9 (library binding)
  1. Discoveries in geography—Juvenile literature. 2. Explorers—Juvenile literature. I. Title.
  G175.G475 2008
  910.9'03—dc22
                                            2007031273

Manufactured in the United States of America

Contents

The Age of Exploration

The Age of **Exploration** is also called the Age of Discovery. It was a period when European countries explored the world. They sent out ships to learn about the world beyond Europe. The Age of Exploration began in the early 1400s and helped shape the world we know today.

However, these Europeans were not the first explorers. People from Asia looking for new lands to settle came to the Americas about 15,000 years ago. In **ancient** times, Egyptians, Greeks, South Pacific islanders, Chinese, and other people explored the world. People have been exploring since the time of the earliest humans.

Spanish explorer Ponce de Leon explored the coast of Florida and many islands in the Caribbean Sea. He was looking for a fountain of youth he had heard about in stories.

1. Why did Europeans make these long trips?

Europeans wanted **spices** from Asia. They used spices to season food and to keep it from rotting. They could get spices from traders, who brought them across land **routes**. However, other countries controlled the land routes. This made the spices very costly. Europeans hoped to find direct ocean routes so they could bring back spices themselves.

2. Why are we doing this?

Europeans also wanted **silk** and other costly goods from Asia. Some Europeans hoped to spread their beliefs to other lands. Others hoped to take control of other lands.

3. Who is paying for all this?

The countries that financed the most explorations were Portugal, Spain, England, and France.

These people are traveling on the Silk Road. The Silk Road was the name for the trade route people took across Asia.

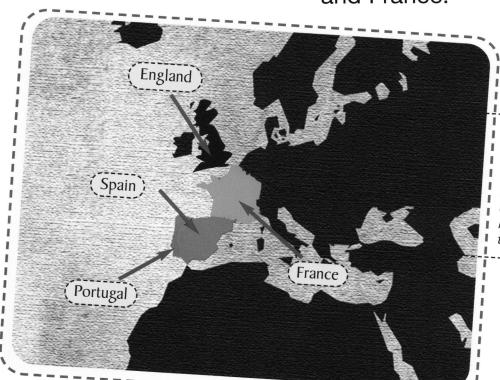

England

Spain

Portugal

France

This map shows Portugal, Spain, England, and France, which were the main countries that paid explorers to look for new lands and new trade routes.

4. Why do they call him the Navigator?

Portugal's Prince Henry wanted to find a sea route around Africa to Asia. He also wanted to learn about Africa and to find gold. Henry sent many **expeditions** down Africa's west coast in the early 1400s. He became known as Prince Henry the **Navigator** because he helped plan the expeditions.

Many ship captains feared going beyond **Cape** Bojador, on Africa's northwest coast. Stories

Cape Bojador

Sierra Leone

This image shows Africa. Cape Bojador is marked in red, and Sierra Leone is marked in orange.

Prince Henry was the son of King John I of Portugal and Philippa of Lancaster, who was the sister of King Henry IV of England. Though Prince Henry was called the Navigator, he never sailed on any of the expeditions he helped plan.

told of sea monsters and water so hot it bubbled. Gil Eanes sailed past Cape Bojador in 1434. This proved the stories were untrue. When Henry died in 1460, Portuguese ships had traveled as far as Sierra Leone.

5. Did you find it?

King John II of Portugal ordered Bartolomeu Dias to find Africa's southern end. Dias left in 1487. He passed the end of Africa without knowing it. He saw he had succeeded after he gave up and turned around to go home. He reached Portugal in 1488 with the news. The king named Africa's tip the Cape of Good Hope.

This is the Cape of Good Hope, in Africa. A cape is a piece of land that sticks out into the ocean and has water on three sides.

6. What did you bring back?

King Manuel I of Portugal ordered Vasco da Gama to sail around Africa to Asia. Da Gama left in 1497. He returned two years later with spices and costly stones.

Vasco da Gama would make three trips around Africa to India in his lifetime. He played a large part in making Portugal an important world power of the time.

7. Would you like an empire?

King Ferdinand and Queen Isabella wanted a Spanish **empire**. An Italian navigator named Christopher Columbus repeatedly asked them to pay for his plan to reach Asia. Finally, they agreed.

Christopher Columbus first started working as a sailor at age 10. He first presented his idea to sail west to Asia to Portugal's king in 1485 but was turned down.

8. Are you sure you can get east by sailing west?

Columbus believed he could reach Asia by sailing west. In 1492, he reached land he thought was part of Asia. This land was really an island in the Caribbean Sea.

Amerigo Vespucci was an Italian businessman, explorer, and mapmaker. He was the first European to think that South America was a new continent, rather than part of Asia.

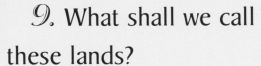

Amerigo Vespucci was an Italian navigator and explorer. He claimed he visited a New World west of Europe in 1497. A German mapmaker believed Vespucci was the first to reach this New World. He named it America on a map, in Vespucci's honor.

Here Columbus is telling the Spanish king and queen of his discoveries in the New World. As part of his deal with them, Columbus asked to be made governor of any lands he found.

Spanish explorers searched for riches in the New World. Juan Ponce de León found gold in Puerto Rico in 1508. In 1513, he reached land he named Florida. Vasco Nuñez de Balboa found gold in Panama in 1513 and became the first European to see the eastern shore of the Pacific Ocean. Hernán Cortés **conquered** the rich Aztec Indians of Mexico in 1521.

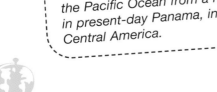

Here Balboa is shown looking at the Pacific Ocean from a mountain in present-day Panama, in Central America.

Ferdinand Magellan believed he could reach Asia by sailing around South America. Magellan died during the trip. However, one of his ships became the first ship to sail around the world!

This is the Strait of Magellan, between the Atlantic Ocean and the Pacific Ocean, which Ferdinand Magellan discovered in South America. A strait is a narrow waterway that goes between two larger bodies of water.

12. Did you say there is a rich Indian empire?

Spanish **conquistador** Francisco Pizarro heard stories about a rich Indian empire. He conquered the Inca Empire in Peru, in 1533, and found much gold and silver.

Francisco Pizarro explored the land on the west coast of South America around Peru. He killed many of the native people in his search for gold and new lands for Spain.

Hernando de Soto and his men explored the southern United States around 1540. They found no gold but became the first Europeans to see the Mississippi River. About the same time, Francisco Vasquez de Coronado and his men explored the southwestern United States. They searched unsuccessfully for seven cities of gold they had heard about. In 1542, Juan Rodriguez Cabrillo and his men were the first Europeans to explore California. They looked for the seven cities of gold, too.

Here conquistador Hernando de Soto and his men see the Mississippi River for the first time and claim it for Spain. De Soto first began exploring the New World in 1514.

14. Should we ask for directions?

English and French explorers unsuccessfully sought the **Northwest Passage**. John Cabot and his son Sebastian tried first. They explored for England around 1500.

15. Who thought it would be so hard?

Giovanni da Verrazano tried unsuccessfully to find the passage for France in 1524. French explorer Jacques Cartier searched in 1534 and 1535. Henry Hudson tried four times between 1607 and 1610. He did not find the passage, though.

Giovanni da Verrazano was an Italian explorer who worked for France. He is best known for exploring North America between South Carolina and Newfoundland.

16. Will you show me around?

Indians helped Samuel de Champlain explore parts of Canada and New York for France. He was the first European to see the lake he named Lake Champlain.

Hudson's ship Half Moon *is shown exploring the river in New York that now bears his name, the Hudson River. Hudson worked for the Dutch East India Company.*

Samuel de Champlain *made his first trip to North America in 1603. He returned many times and helped start many French settlements in Canada.*

Portuguese explorers of the early 1400s carried **slaves** as well as gold from Africa to Portugal. The first slaves came to the New World in the early 1500s. The first slaves arrived in the United States in 1619.

This picture shows a Dutch ship that has arrived in Jamestown, Virginia, in 1619, with slaves for sale.

18. What was the trip like?

The trip from Africa to the New World was called the Middle Passage. The ships' captains packed slaves so close together they could not move. Many slaves died during the trip.

19. Can we be friends?

Explorers and Native Americans were often friendly at first. However, sicknesses brought by explorers killed many Indians. Indians began to fight as more people came and took their land.

Here Henry Hudson trades with friendly Native Americans on the banks of the present-day Hudson River.

20. Is there anything left to discover?

The Age of Exploration ended in the early 1600s. European countries had begun to build settlements in the New World by that time.

That did not mean there was nothing left to explore. French explorers Louis Jolliet and Jacques Marquette traveled part of the Mississippi River in 1673. A French explorer called La Salle traveled the whole Mississippi River in 1682.

American explorers Meriwether Lewis and William Clark explored the land west of the Mississippi River between 1804 and 1806. Norway's Roald Amundsen completed the first trip through the Northwest Passage in 1906.

Glossary

ancient (AYN-shent) Very old, from a long time ago.

cape (KAYP) A point of land that sticks out into the water.

conquered (KON-kerd) Overcame by force of arms.

conquistador (kon-KEES-tuh-dor) A Spanish soldier, or fighter, who explored and conquered large areas of the Americas between 1500 and 1600.

empire (EM-pyr) A large area controlled by one ruler.

expeditions (ek-spuh-DIH-shunz) Trips for a special purpose.

exploration (ek-spluh-RAY-shun) Travel through little-known land.

navigator (NA-vuh-gay-ter) A person who uses maps, the stars, or special tools to travel in a ship.

Northwest Passage (NORTH-west PA-sij) A passage through which one could sail between the North Atlantic Ocean and the Pacific Ocean.

routes (ROOTS) The paths a person takes to get somewhere.

silk (SILK) Cloth made from thread made only by certain worms.

slaves (SLAYVZ) People who are "owned" by another person and forced to work for him or her.

spices (SPYS-ez) Seasonings from certain plants that are used to give taste to food.

Index

A
Age of Discovery, 4
America(s), 4, 13
Asia, 4, 6, 8, 11–12,
    15

C
Cape of Good
    Hope, 10
Chinese, 4
Cortés, Hernán, 14

E
Egyptians, 4
Europe, 4, 13

G
Greeks, 4

N
Northwest Passage,
    18, 22

P
Prince Henry the
    Navigator, 8–9

S
silk, 6
slaves, 20–21
South Pacific
    islanders, 4
spices, 6, 11

Web Sites

Due to the changing nature of Internet links, PowerKids Press has developed an online list of Web sites related to the subject of this book. This site is updated regularly. Please use this link to access the list:
www.powerkidslinks.com/20his/explor/